MEDEA

MEDEA
© 2017 Catherine Theis

Published by Plays Inverse Press
New York, NY
www.playsinverse.com

ISBN 13: 978-0-9914183-6-7

First Printing: February 2017
Cover design by Megan J. Pryce
Page design by Tyler Crumrine
Printed in the U.S.A.

PLAYS
INVERSE

MEDEA

CATHËRINE THEIS

Plays Inverse Press
New York, NY
2017

for Aaron

On the windy mountain ridge
shrill voices of girls
echo to the beat all night
of feet dancing.

— Euripides, *The Heraklaidai*

INTRODUCTION

I've always been interested in Greek drama, in the use of myth, and in how the Romans reimagined Greek ideas. Because of these interests, I'm drawn to how voice (music) and tone (quality, pitch, and strength) work in a poem or play. I'm interested in rhetoric, in performance, in all-night rituals. I want my work to have the force of something spilling out, uncontainable: either leaking from a mask or booming from a leafy treetop. It's that balance of wildness of emotion and language, coupled with the restraint that comes through form and grammar, that is interesting to me.

This particular play is a retelling of the Medea story set in Montana, or some mountain place. My approach for *MEDEA* includes sound-poems, or soundscapes, voice dialogues *sul telefono*, as well as traditional scenes. There are a few instances where the language breaks down so much we must discover a new language in order to be heard. What is bracketed speech if not total ruin-destruction, spoken from the underside of voice? So also, The Milky Way is a character in this play, and I imagine her as a troupe of dancers, a true moving galaxy. Medea happens to be an amateur photographer at this point in her life, and so her photographs appear as important time markers of the play's dramatic intensity and should be projected as backdrop. Indeed, the play's final catastrophes (the poisoned fall of lovers, the flames) should include THE REFRAIN, or "how to consolidate the material, make it consistent, so it can harness the unthinkable, invisible, nonsonorous forces."[1] Medea wants to join with the world, to meld with it. Let's let her

---

[1] See Deleuze and Guattari. *A Thousand Plateaus: Capitalism and Schizophrenia* (University of Minnesota, 1987).

do that—see what falls away. Starlight will need to be represented onstage more than just as stage light. Included are the palate-cleansing satyr plays haunted by the ghost of Duchamp. *The Satyr Plays* are like giant paintings, created on-site with wine-paint, specific for each performance. Their purpose is to brighten moods after Medea's story. Remember *Medea* calls for Bach, a chorus of flames speaking in brightest voice: it calls to burn down its own theatre doors.

Catherine Theis
Santa Monica, California

CHARACTERS

MEDEA
HUSBAND
SISTER
INNKEEPER
MISTRESS
THE MILKY WAY
A CHORUS OF FLAMES

SET

The set includes a living room (complete with a TV),
a kitchen,
a windy mountain road,
a red Alfa Romeo curving up the mountain road,
a grand lodge (with 3 small cabins) alongside a running
stream,
the Milky Way,
a golden trapdoor,
and a tennis court hung with white flowers.

NOTES

Medea and her Husband should be played as though they have known each other for at least a century. Medea should not be combative or quick to anger. She wears a small gold pendant in the shape of a diadem on her neck, small pearls at the five points of crown.

The Alfa Romeo should be a model from the late 1970s, and not in the best condition. It needs to have been driven in and around Mount Etna, preferably in the small town of Taormina. Please, only one candy bar in the glove compartment. Candy bar must have nougat, almonds, and caramel. (Check at specialty stores that sell UK-imported goods.)

The chorus of flames is like a raging river, is like the "bloody tyrant time."

The set should suggest "mood" rather than true background. However, piles of ice and snow may be wheel-barrowed in for the second and third movements.

Fresh white flowers a necessity at the play's close. Medea's sister a dark-haired beauty.

 The play should be performed with an unwilling audience.

MEDEA

PROLOGUE

Darkness. A beam of moonlight
falls on a woman
in a navy blue cocktail dress.
She steps out in front
of a stone colonnade,
wearing stilettos
with oversized bows
fastened at the heels.
She carries a torch,
an eternal flame.

SISTER

Deep in windstorm,
our tragedy begins.
Medea, happy as a heretic,

exiled in shadow.
Her scalloped neckline
dotted in springtime.

White blossoms in a row.
Start with the spiritual,
go on from there.

Among the ruins
pretending grave,
Medea stands near

a colonnade,
a blood wound.
The wind begins to blow.

Her imperfect interlude.
Her imperfect Chorus.
Husband as camera lens:

a missing rib, a world
off its axis. As her sister,
I knew his refrain

would be a load
too heavy to bear.
The wind drops stones.

What of his Greek birth?
What of the cold sea air?
What of my pity?

What of my fear?
I walk the monologue
of a fierce natural world,

a layer of smoked salt
hand-packed into hot
ground. Nothing ever

private in an ancient city.
Trusting in chariots.
Trusting in the impulse

of right & wrong.
Trusting in a tragic stage,
a platform between heaven & hell.

I wish my sister such fierce
love never knew. Chipping.
Clicking. Grinding

bones into stones.
Bones without eyes.
If I could peel off the flesh

from his bones, naked
bones without eyes.
I speak a tournament

of wills, a sour-sweetness.
Cut these words
from my throat.

They do not belong here.

FIRST MOVEMENT

SCENE 1

A young woman stretches out
on an expensive white couch.
A Western on TV. Fire in the fireplace.
Nearby, her Husband signs checks.
Stacks of unpaid bills surround them.

MEDEA

All I want to do is drink beer
and float. If I'm lucky, I can choreograph
my own fall, my own birthright.
Two types of theatre-goers:
those who are on time and those
who are not. "Live in hiding,"
the philosopher says.
Would you try a chocolate-covered
ant if I offered one to you?

HUSBAND

What do you mean, try?

He does not look up from the checkbook.

MEDEA

Try as in to eat, to slice
with divine teeth!
To masticate with back molars!
To eat where others
have eaten and enjoyed.

Her arms above her head in a wild totem pose.

HUSBAND

You make no sense sometimes, Medea.

MEDEA

She speaks directly to the audience.

My Husband likes to do this—
repeat his experiences.
I mean, who actually likes
watching a Western they've seen
258 times? He's trying to maximize
his happiness. Obviously, he's not
going to win. No one wins
against Pain. He's been fighting
Pain a lot lately. His face muscles
built up against Pain's prickling.
I notice the difference, even
if my Husband doesn't
appreciate his new cheekiness.

At the commercial, she places a cowboy hat over her face.

I sleep under a saguaro tree.
With snakes curling around
my pelvis, I'm the eternal tree.

Can I lick the stamps for you?

HUSBAND

Of course, sweetie.

He hands her a roll of stamps.

Have we ever seen this movie before?

MEDEA

Are you kidding me?
I can't be expected to watch television
every night until I'm eighty.
The net's been too high for too long.
You've been playing to my disadvantage,
my weedy appetite out of hand.
I can't be expected to reinvigorate
two thousand years of thinking by myself.

HUSBAND

Medea! What's with you lately?

MEDEA

I feel restless.
Will you tie this blindfold on me?

HUSBAND

No, I will not.
I'm trying to pay these bills.

MEDEA

What is your true gift to me?
I want it evenly. Without
examining entrails or reading
tea leaves, I want it now.

She gets up, stands behind her Husband,
making a gun with her thumb and forefinger.
She slowly aims the gun at her Husband,
then switches aim toward her own head.
She pulls the trigger. The flames rise higher.

HUSBAND

Why don't we go on a road trip?
I think we're going to get more snow
this weekend. Might be fun to find a cabin.

MEDEA

Can we go to the hot springs?

HUSBAND

Sure. Why not?

MEDEA

Okay, I'll start packing.

HUSBAND

I'll clean the car.

MEDEA

Why do you always clean the car
before we go on a trip? Makes no sense
to me, we're just going to dirty it.

HUSBAND

I like starting trips with a clean car.

MEDEA

Fine. Whatever you like.
I'm going to start packing.

HUSBAND

Don't forget the camera—
you forgot it last time.

> *Medea pulls out a suitcase from underneath the couch.*
> *She plays a Lou Reed record while she packs.*
> *She continues packing, and practices*
> *air guitar on her thigh.*
> *At one point, she holds up a pair of pants*
> *and smells the crotch.*

Scene 2

Medea & Husband

The story of how we met a familiar one.
A kind of out-of-doors thinking.

Imagined and illustrated by Shakespeare,
explained by Emerson, but judged by

Steiner as "moral infirmity" or "active vice."
Our chorus a "lyric tapestry" in overdrive.

No clue sex expected as fair reply.
No clue accepted as unexpected

in some cases, no clue you couldn't say
rule as a way of speaking your funny bone.

The nerve of some! No clue I couldn't be
the center of attention or the smarter one.

No clue bodies burned in blue notes
on the patio at night, *foie gras et Sauternes*,

a private wish beamed into exposed
plenitude. No clue a false blue leapt in pursuit

of first sex, second sex. No clue we could close
our eyes in the Forest of Arden, Duke scene.

No clue what your letters looked like in the dark,
hanging lanterns, perfumed bark. Notable clue

that when it's too sweet, it's rancid for sure.
See earlier aubade. No clue smashed lips.

No clue smoke in limestone caves.
Keep my mouth sweet, bruised, all color

raced to lips, flushed—no clue theft of foot,
theft of lands, no clue car door cavern

close. No clue you slipped a tiny Polaroid
into my wallet, parrots nesting in the palms.

No clue your lips spear dove into a bloody
reef trashed in smashed remnants of chariot

wheel debris. Wreckage of stories spun in deceit.
O how we longed for fate to intervene!

SECOND MOVEMENT

SCENE 1

Medea and her Husband drive up
the mountain road in a red Alfa Romeo.
The snow is snowing lovingly down on them.
What is there not to love in this giant world?

MEDEA

Will you teach me to drive?

HUSBAND

Sure, if you want. But not today.

MEDEA

(under her breath) And not tomorrow either.

HUSBAND

What was that? I couldn't hear you.

MEDEA

Oh, nothing! Just saying how close
we must be. Honey, please don't speed.
We could slip off, and no one would know.

> *Medea fiddles with her camera. The gallery full*
> *of rattlesnakes, char, smoke scenes, desert cacti.*

HUSBAND

Medea, I'm in perfect control.
But these mountains! Such wild country!
Would you protect me
from the mountain lions' fire-breath?

MEDEA

You know my loyalty.
Look, I brought the good champagne.

> *Two trails down to the hot springs.*
> *An empty champagne bottle,*
> *its orange label against the snowdrift.*

Scene 2

Medea and her Husband back in the car.
Their hair is wet. Their faces flushed with vigor.
They kiss a bit before the engine starts.

Medea & Husband

Past a bridge and frozen brook named
after Lewis and Clark, our car speeds past
the "Snowmobilers Only" sign to catch Helios,
grandfather-god of the setting sun.
Down into the four o'clock valley—
our car stops, sinks, breaks crust—
four feet of packed snow.
Sign reads: Killed Colt Bridge.
"I bet this is where Lewis and Clark
ate their colt." Our car's tires spin
in place. Sportsmanship. We sit in the car,
laughing at our luck. "I have one Mars bar
left. I'll share it with you." We take turns
saying this to one another. It's funny.
Almost dinnertime, how good
we must taste to the roving others—
see how easily the *I* becomes the *we*?

An hour passes.

Tires spin and spin.
We stand around
like unlit birthday candles
in white cake frosting
waiting to be rescued.

Another hour passes.

Tires spin, and spin, skidding
nowhere in the snow.
This time not just our car's
but the ranger's more giant ones.
We're advised to spend the night.

Scene 3

An image of a bloodied decapitated elk's head
on a truck's grill appears in the sky
above an alpine Lodge.
Medea and her Husband enter the Lodge's bar.

Medea & Husband

We've always wanted to stay here.
Here, look at this!

> *Photograph of a car stuck in snow.*
> *Another photograph of a wolf behind a pine tree.*

Innkeeper

Certainly a good reason.
Better luck tomorrow morning, I'm sure.
We'll get you set up in Milky Way
Cabin No. 3. A little dinner first?

Medea & Husband

That would be lovely.
Do you have any huckleberry buckle?

Innkeeper

Yes, we do. Huckleberry here,
huckleberry there. Huckleberry,
huckleberry everything.
What would you like to drink?

Medea & Husband

Whiskey. Can we also order two steaks?
We're starving!

Innkeeper

Sure thing. I'll let the kitchen know.
Potatoes and butter and bread, all okay?

Medea & Husband

Yes, please. Thanks.

> *Happy as honeymooners,*
> *they settle into the rhythm of the Lodge.*
> *Two hunters silently smoke*
> *at the other end of the bar, eyeing the couple.*

SCENE 4

THE MILKY WAY

A wood-burning stove
is theirs for the stoking.
Given a private cottage
on the perimeter
of the Lodge's land,
huckleberry here, huckle
-berry there, world stained
in order. Full and happy,
Medea and Husband roll
into a single twin bed.
Only when three dogs howl
do they get up and inspect
*******   the night sky / hot-white ladled *********
*stars **************
poured just for them.

MEDEA

This trip has been a lot of fun.
So many mountains.

She exhales smoke, passes the joint to her Husband.

HUSBAND

Yes, it has.

MEDEA

I think I really needed to get out of town.

HUSBAND

Me too.

He kisses her shoulder. The moonlight spills on his forehead.

MEDEA

I suddenly feel very awake.

HUSBAND

Medea, what is it?

MEDEA

I want to remember everything.
I want eyewitnesses too.
The blind-out spot replaced
with a knowing eye. Remember
how I told you it was an accident,
but no one believed me? How I
was chased out of town like a criminal?
It was only supposed to be deep-dark
sleep, only a cloak of Death
still warming their tiny bodies.

HUSBAND

Right, and then Euripides came along
and wrote that play.

MEDEA

And, I can't prove it…but Aristophanes might.
I mean, someone stole into my study
and meddled with my herbs.
Remedy for a toothache the easiest!
I've administered those to countless children.
And didn't I suffer?

HUSBAND

Well, what about it?

MEDEA

A couple of weeks ago, I went to the doctor's.

HUSBAND

Why, what's wrong?

MEDEA

Nothing is wrong per se, but I was late.

HUSBAND

Oh, I see.

> *He turns away. In bed—awake—*
> *both ship-packed like silver herrings—transatlantic sail*
> *until the stars burn out.*
> *They wait for morning cold.*
> *The icicles downward drop and drip.*

The Milky Way

Above a broad field
whose wheat burns bare—

days of heaven,
nights of deception
where grasshoppers swarm.

See A. Kiefer's painting titled
Die Milchstrasse (1985-87).

Medea

That's a great one. Call it
"Catastrophe of Ecstatic Reverie,"
the overturning of rational thought.
But I forget how you came to be.
Your identity as a spiral galaxy?

The Milky Way

Heracles, of both heaven
and earth, sucks on Hera's breast,
whose milk of kindness
sprays a starry chest.

And so we are thus born—
a spray of grace
across the nightly firmament.

Medea

Your glowing strands cast
filament after filament.

In the cataract of disaster,
a down-rushing of forms.
A curtain fall of blue flowers.

The Milky Way

A troupe of dancers.
A garland of white roses.
A choir, a classic outline
of marble pillars.
We court, we kingly court
refrains of carnage and decay.
We cannot say what moves
your thoughts, Medea.
Helios knows, we've tried.
Perhaps it's just beyond
the forward fracture
of Time itself.
....
        ....
....
....
        ....
....

What follows are directions for dance.
The Milky Way should be allowed
one grand piano, a choreographer,
and a bottle of wine.

DELUSION
CATASTROPHE
TRANCE
DELIRIUM
HERITAGE

PASTNESS OF PAST TIME
RUMOR
MEND THE RUINS
ONE LAST TIME
IS IT TOO LATE
ECHO
FIRE FLAMES
WHAT HAPPENED
ROMAN RUINS
URN DANCE
AMONG THE RUINS

The Milky Way

    Private cottage territories
* * * * *

       reclaimed
        journal form
  Huckleberry here
          huckle
     -berry there,
      world stained   * * *
in order   Medea & Husband
    bedrolled   a single twin
twinned belts
   Gemini **

Night sky
      hot-white   Night coverlet

  ladled stars   **BRIGHT ACCIDENT**
**
   ***

  ship-packed herrings   transatlantic sail

Medea Speaks

Eyewitnesses   [The blind-out spot]
replaced [knowing
eye]

   [sun] [sun] [sun] Remember

It was an accident?

Chased out of town [a criminal]

Then, Euripides
         [oh yeah, him] [that play] [I'm going to be late]

                  [Meddled
with my bulbs] I can't prove it

Remedies: toothaches: stomach cramps: insomnia: heatstroke

[countless children]   [including my own]
         Administer

   I suffered [centuries] [centuries] [centuries]

at the Shrub of Fate

THIRD MOVEMENT

SCENE 1

Medea and her Husband wake to the silence
of snow. White trapdoors.
Cream in the milkmaid's bucket.
They walk over toward the main Lodge.
Decorated in antler heads, a breakfast room.

HUSBAND

Coffee?

MEDEA

Yes, I would love a cup of coffee
and a croissant, but I would settle
for cardamom toast. God, I miss
Sweden! So civilized, do you know
that in Sweden…

HUSBAND

Medea!

> *He grabs her arm before*
> *she crosses the threshold.*
> *Their faces lit in a strange glow.*
> *Inside, the kitchen engulfed in flames.*

MEDEA

Fire!

HUSBAND

Run the faucets!

MEDEA

Probably some pots in the kitchen.

HUSBAND

Fill those up. We need to get water
to the roof.

MEDEA

There's a ladder by the back door.

HUSBAND

Where? Oh, here.

> *He positions the ladder outside*
> *in a snowbank, against the Lodge.*
> *One pot, two pot up the burning roof.*
> *Water runs down, catches nothing.*

MEDEA

This isn't working.

> *In the distance, the stream wails audibly.*

HUSBAND

This is your midnight pilgrimage, isn't it?

You did this.
The penance and burning of scorched earth.
The vertigo behind the rising flames.
But isn't this destruction all a little too easy?

The Chorus of Flames Speaks

STROPHE

Smoke. Smoke

Smoke Smoke Smoke
   where shaft continues
      to ceiling to roof
then   Smoke
  Smoke   Smoke willowing out
     catching wind match smoke
    windsmoke   ghost
   Years tar
Pine paper pasture   faster the smoke

Roof's a good place to start
     Dry roast, dry rusk
of toast   breakfast burned

      Memories stacked in
Proustian description
    Poisoned children
All those unborn

  My eyes burn

Flaming diadem melts skin to bone

       Why did you do it?

ANTISTROPHE

   Medea enters with large oversized
   sheets of parchment paper.
   She fans the paper at the Chorus of Flames.

I lost all patience.

EPODE

Patience is
a whore town.
A sari wrapped all wrong.
A monogram used in choral songs.
Patience is a pent-up rage scouring
earth for enchantresses.
Structures collapse.
Inner and outer ash.
Generous water always flows.
Orange with blue, red with blue,
blue-orange with blue. Smoke as veils,
veils smoked in the smokehouse
like homemade sausages.
The river always with a trapdoor,
Medea knows. The place razed.
Her plan to tidy up at curtain's close.
Horses drowned in the river.
A telephone buried in the snow.
To leave this Husband just like the last.
Habit-forming, we rise higher.

> *Why did you do it?*
> *What do you know of creation?*

ANTISTROPHE

The cannon must be fired
at exactly the right time.

The tension of one long take
or the outlaw turns classic.

The white passage
of a chipped ancient sculpture.

When normal translations fail,
"unfamiliar" is perhaps the point.

The freedom of the field
or thirteen curtain calls.

When Saturn devours his children,
no one calls the cops. Goya chops

holes in doors.
Boring hole after hole after hole in doors.

Task of the translator
is to measure lumber. To paint.

"I'm only going as far as there…"
(points to a white space on the next page)

Conversing with the dead
or sticking my foot in the campfire.

I can feel the difference between
inside and outside pyramid stones.

A flame of fire. A sword.
My "archives of grief"

confident as the rock,
confident as the ocean.

So is this what *it* is?
A fire speaking within us?

You, my Imperfect Chorus, stage
yourselves closer to the devouring,

awake, dented into morning,
find the brightness of wound.

And when the wine darkens
a terror begins—*terroir*, a roar,

misused, my experience
is theatrical, not actual.

All-Speech

[midnight pilgrimage] [penance burning]
[scorched earth] [vertigo]
[rising flames] [destruction] [easy]
[river] [trapdoor]
[children-closed]
[tidy up] [curtain's close]
[river] [horses drown]
[telephone] [buried snow]
[habit-forming] [leave]
[walk] [woods] [photographs]
[fire ire]

Husband Speaks

Violence is primitive
but widespread.
A gallon of milk
to water the weeds.
Medea is carried across
a wooded lot.
Her silver sandals,
perfect slipper moons.
The smell of burning.
Our insides rich
with talkings and imaginings.
The window shade its own puppet
theatre—Lear Head and Outlaw.
Words can mean anything:
truce, truce, truce.
She carries a briefcase
but her body means,
"withhold judgment."

SCENE 5

In the distance, the Lodge engulfed in flames.
Husband walks to a payphone
on the other side of the road.
He dials a number.

HUSBAND

Hi, it's me…what? No, I don't think so.
We're always in the middle of ourselves…
…just a jejune example, an after-image
gone too far…No. Yes, of course I miss you.
I can't talk long.

    He shakes his head.

Yes, the Headless Woman onstage.
Did you see her as something more
than illusion? I'm sorry, I didn't realize…

Did I inflict pain?

    Pause.

Did I inflict pain?

    Pause.

Did I inflict pain?

    Pause.

I thought you liked it.

    Pause.

Yes, you told me you did.

Pause.

Strange fruit?

Pause.

How much per pound?

Pause.

How much this pain?

Pause.

How little she strains.

Pause.

From the poplar trees?

Pause.

You know I love Dover Beach.
I'll take you there someday.
There's a fabulous café
on the British side of the street
where the croissants are
just like Calais. What? Ah, huh.
Time works us against us.

> *Medea appears, walking past
> the Husband on the payphone.
> They nod to one another.*

He points to his watch and smiles.
She continues down to the river.

MEDEA

Time works us against us.
Like the way a circle moves in origin,
collapsing celestial into the oceanic.
The living power of the imagination
seems too bright at times, though
we cannot doubt the role of the eternal.
Like the newlywed pining for a croissant
in Calais, or how we jump island ferries,
making merry our marriage bed in the flea,
intermezzo of refrain. Here I go.

> *Medea opens a trapdoor into the riverbed.*
> *She holds an old photograph of Husband,*
> *looking down into the hole.*

I'm already asleep when my Husband lifts up
the blanket. The cold hits my body like the wet,
dark mouth of a ghost. Silver darlings, the bobby
stick brings reason after bruises, the pent-up rage
of England keeps the search in the bathtub, mermaids
alive in muck. Shape of the London river, a V
in my tree branch vision. The ghost vanishes, flowing
out like a river into the ocean. But it is my Husband
who smells like wood smoke, cigarette smoke, whiskey—
or bourbon, I can't tell—ginger ale, marshmallows,
chocolate, coffee, hot dogs, pickles, yellow mustard
not Dijon, sage, white lilies, saltwater, potato chips,
lobster, rosemary, sandstone, forest pine, a mountain
ridge lit by the new moon, Clint's green poncho
of scratchy wool, corn husks warming in a corn field,

coffee ice cream, the mystery perfume sample with
the faded gray lettering, my mother's ragù of beef shank
and pork shoulder, whitefish from the fish boil
near a Wisconsin lake, sails of a sailboat,
almond milk, apples from the farmers' market,
chicken cutlets, my feisty black dog, the inside
of my red coat pocket, turkey stuffing, eggnog, pine
trees again. I open my eyes in the dark room but see
nothing. "Are there any bats tonight?" "Plenty,"
he says, and kisses my neck. We are both drunk.
This is the fun part. Cultivating an island is hard work.
The sea encroaches, the sun is too hot.
The green needs more water, then less,
then a professional gardener must be
called to correct the novice's mistakes.
I can't fall back asleep. I wait for water.
But there's pressure inside the mountain.
I'm afraid it's transforming into a volcano.
All the birds have flown. Even the birds know
it's time to head out on sulfur fume.
Where do you put bold voices?
The wish for bold speech never escapes me.

   Medea falls down.

A small rundown cabin, one of three.
Bedspread of pastel yellows and greens.
A six-pack of cheap beer near the TV.
An attractive woman reapplies lipstick.
Voice gives itself over to gesture.

MISTRESS

Flowers are unbuttoning themselves
on my blouse.

HUSBAND

No, those are my hands, silly.

He runs his hands up and down
her torso, touching breasts.

MISTRESS

Who's silly?

HUSBAND

You are.

MISTRESS

No, I'm intuitive with fire.
I'm the firewatcher in this couple.

HUSBAND

Fire is intimate, is it not?

He kisses her.

MISTRESS

*She breaks free
from his mouth.*

The "art of kindling"
is a great skill to have.
Also fish in my dreams.

They kiss.

HUSBAND

How many did you see?

MISTRESS

Belvedere. Belfiore. Beautiful flowers.
Fire in my dreams.

HUSBAND

First sign of reverie?

MISTRESS

Eggs cooking in milky-white ashes.
Fire hot, it bleeds.

HUSBAND

How many eggs?

MISTRESS

Of course there were two, silly!
One for you, and one for me.

HUSBAND

That wasn't what I was asking.

MISTRESS

I know. But still a concern.
Tailoring a talk inside the break.

HUSBAND

I'm sorry. I don't understand you.

MISTRESS

That's okay. I don't think you ever did.

HUSBAND

Why would you say something like that?
I care about you. I'm here, aren't I?

He opens up a beer.

Do you know how dangerous this is?

MISTRESS

I think she already knows.
She was looking at me funny

when she picked Charlie up
from school last week.

HUSBAND

Oh, God. I told you to leave that alone.

MISTRESS

Don't get mad at me.
I didn't do anything. Was
just on playground duty.

HUSBAND

I'll figure something out.
She hardly likes being around me
anymore.

MISTRESS

That's great for me, I guess.

> *She rolls her eyes.*
> *He grabs her and kisses her.*
> *Through the window,*
> *flames are visible.*

FOURTH MOVEMENT

SCENE 1

In Medea's kitchen. A large sign
hangs above the sink. It reads:

If you dirty a dish
You wash that fish
Off the plate or else!

She sits at a large table
folding pink napkins.
Persian-embroidered.
A camera at her side.

MEDEA

Prevention better than tragedy?
Is that even possible?
I'd rather be an atomic flower.
Pretty, but self-imploding.

> *She raises her voice.*

Are you listening to me?

HUSBAND

> *He steps into the kitchen,*
> *carrying a tennis racquet.*
> *He smokes a tiny razor joint.*

What? Sorry, didn't hear a word you said.

Takes a tennis ball out of his pocket,
spins it with one hand.

I'm going out.

MEDEA

Never mind. The other night
I dreamed you were going
on a blind date.

Camera clicks the quick retreat of snakehead.

HUSBAND

That is funny. You're a strange bird.
Did you get a haircut or something?

MEDEA

No, but I'm due for one soon.
Hey, hold still. Let me take a photo
of you with your racquet.
I want to remember the good times.

Husband poses.

Notes

1. Breakup Scene with House Plants (civilized)
2. Breakup Scene with Fire (barbaric, not successful last time)
3. Breakup Scene in Alfa Romeo (too Italian)
4. Breakup Scene Near Swimming Pool (too unlike them)
5. Breakup Scene in Africa (too exilesque)
6. Breakup Scene in the Library (too obvious)
7. Breakup Scene in Coffee Shop (too cliché)
8. Breakup Scene in Bar (too dangerous)
9. Breakup Scene on the Front Porch (the old oak)
10. Breakup Scene on the Golf Course (too insect-like)

SCENE 3

Medea and Sister at the table.
A vase of irises between them.

SISTER

Medea, I've never seen you like this.

MEDEA

Stuck, stuck—a fucking weed in muck.
No open door in the riverbed.
No fire, no lyre, no Milky Way.

SISTER

Without having realized, you've settled
in this god-forsaken Western place,
smelling of cow shit, reeking
of sulfur weeds. Leave him!

MEDEA

I know, but I can't. I don't know
how. How did I end up with no
future, no past, no present?
No children but with somebody else's?

SISTER

Be bandanna black to blind luck,
body-double stand-up.
Spit new seeds between your legs.

A cell phone starts ringing.

You've been unhappy this past year.
Medea, your phone is ringing.

MEDEA

That's not my phone.

SISTER

Well, it's not my phone.
God, is he still smoking pot?

MEDEA

Yeah, it's a problem.

SISTER

Does he smoke every day?

MEDEA

Yeah, the other morning, I found
him sitting in the car rolling joints.
Style, the special organ
we all want to suck.

The cell phone rings again.

Who is calling him twice in a row?

Medea looks puzzled.

·

SISTER

What should we do for dinner?

MEDEA

I don't recognize this number.
They left a long message, though.

SISTER

Let's listen to it.

MEDEA

That wouldn't be right.

SISTER

What? You're his wife.
You have every right.

Medea listens to the message.
After a minute, her face cracks in pain.

Medea? Medea?…

MEDEA

She sighs deeply.

Here's the plan: kitchen as lab
-oratory, then delivery of a
lemonade liquor. Languidly
at first he'll drink, hot, over

-heated. Ripe with vigor
his world will reappear,
relit from within. I'll use love
to further love and bind those
two adulterers in whatever
misery or bitter sweetness
the gods decree. This time
I won't be to blame! My fire
extinguished but punishment
all the same. If it's love he wants,
it's love he shall get. For me,
a flask of first-beginning.

SCENE 4

Medea and her sister camp out
near the tennis courts of a neighborhood
park. Hidden in greenery, they wait
for the lovers to meet.

While the mood should be intense,
both are enveloped in a sisterly sweetness.

SISTER

I've missed you these last few years.

MEDEA

Have I really been far from you?

SISTER

I hardly ever see you.
If I do, it's because I visit.
You don't answer your phone.

MEDEA

I've been preoccupied,
the restlessness of selfish living.

SISTER

I'm not here to judge.

She kisses Medea.

Look! He's here!

An agile horse,
canteen in hand,
poison lemonade
freshly made!

MEDEA

Always looked so good in white.

> *Her camera clicks*
> *an iambic line*
> *of remembered time in love.*

SISTER

Is that her? Oh my god, she looks
like you! Not as pretty, of course.

> *The two figures collide and kiss.*
> *Medea's heart obliterates.*

MEDEA (UNDER ERASURE)

I'm dead serious ~~when I say all I want to do is drink beer and eat stinky cheese that smells and~~ **looks like dead matter** ~~from inside an old man's nose until my middle bloats and the gas in my middle creates enough momentum that I fall off the couch, and onto the floor.~~ **Off with his head!** ~~If~~ **I'm lucky,** ~~I can choreograph my fall just right so my~~ **pretty little head** ~~lands right on the floor cushions. If I'm not so lucky, the~~ **karma whipsmarts!** ~~me so fast,~~ **my face catches** ~~the corner of the coffee table and I bleed a little on the rug. Blood,~~ **blood. In** ~~the evening, blood appeals to me. The day like a black crow, gouging~~ **my eyes** ~~with its bloodied beak.~~

71

My ~~husband has other designs, which I'll explain in~~ **minute,** ~~but all I want to do is~~ **relax** ~~and watch the national evening news. Or look at the insects~~ **in my glass jar.** ~~Consider and~~ **float.** ~~The only real civilized way to unwind~~ **after a long day.** ~~My fondness for inaction.~~ **"Live in hiding,"** ~~Epicurus says to the philosopher, not because he thinks the philosopher is some stupid idiot who cannot~~ **resist the temptations** ~~of regular life, but because~~ **he understands the fruitfulness** ~~of seclusion,~~ **the garden grass** ~~smoked in pleasure. The dialogue only visible to the insects.~~ **Would you try** ~~a chocolate-covered ant~~ **if I offered one to you?**

Canteen

canteen-kiss
a potion
list
public mist
stitching-stench
/ / / / / /intemperate
flame
double
\ \ \ \ \dealing
burn
deceit
adulterous-two
tap a root
lemon juice
rotten-tooths
bodies
dead

[[[[[[fallen]]]]]]

CADERE

Medea Speaks Her Future

Imagine the shadowless figure
of your lover
as he stands
  before you
    limitless immortal
& you the same
caught in noons
  of contradictions
your breath
a perfect garden
   temperature
 flower-kiss breaking

static
   sunshine
    across lips?

Scene 7

A tavern. A spotlight on Medea.
She reads from The Letters of Medea, *her new book.*
An orange tree realigns its arm toward the sun.

Medea

Hello, everyone. Thanks for coming.
I just want to read a short section
from the new book.
It's from the middle part,
where things turn less lethal
though more unpredictable.
And thank you to my lost
Husband for showing me
in unbloodied instruction
how to roof-top dialogue
without tyranny's fire.
I am monstrously in your debt.

> *She clears her throat. A one-way bell rings. The taste of*
> *iron passing quickly.*

Dear Friends,

Nothing violent in this town.
Fortune's ruinous blasts are not violet here.
The hills soft with mead flowers
and musk-musk berries.
The whole scenery makes me feel pleasantly hungry,
but not so vivid as to make one *ravenous*.
Make no mistake, the underplot dutifully mown:
hunger and rage. And so I wait.
In my closet, fourteen sheer blouses—
all very expensive and not mine.

Funny, I don't like white blouses.
Either a wish, or a counterwish.
I prefer my robes black and sooty
since I can't stop the burning
in my own bodycentury.
Nothing is ever an accident,
the bad fit of creative force,
the metal gate, the sliding shackle.
I killed, I may kill again.
But for now, choreograph me
into the trees' canopy—
pine needle feet in loam-top brush.
Liar, wormweed—I drink what I please,
my new life unprotected by the gods
but swarmed in butterflies.
I do miss the snow,
the lovely cool stream—
the mountains!
I never come the same way twice.
My sister knows this.

In immortal ecstatic fire,
Medea

Medea's Sister Speaks (An Epilogue)

There's a stage inside her

a stage no one has ever walked across
even I haven't been there before

at the back courtyard
at the theatre of Dionysus
where bougainvillea
cascades down her tan & toned shoulders

bushed out magenta pink
overhang lowers a hulled lip

But every so often
I catch a glimpse

      O my sister! O my joy!

of her walking the garden alone
roses blooming from her legs & hips

I'd carry your baby
I'd carry your baby

She smiles, and asks, Remember how I was left?

    spider bites
   tracked across
my right breast

A dry riverbed,
silver crack of ice water—

THE
SATYR
PLAYS

CHARACTERS

BIG BEAR SATYR
LITTLE HUNTER SATYR
RED BULL SATYR
THORN & HORN SATYR

SET

Onstage is a tomb, from which smoke rises.
Vine-shoots trailing off its limestone language.
The Satyrs reminisce of first beginnings.

Braving Fire

*All the Satyrs sit down in a circle. They open wine barrels,
shirttails drenched in wine. Weak wine, weak beliefs, the sun
high above the lemon grove.*

ALL: The stone sharpened by tambourine-fire
   Drink up, drink up, how lovely to not belong
   To the little set, the little clan, the crab legs
   scuttling up
   The paintings fall out of the rock
   White chalk
   Desire leaves us, comes back
   Leaves us again
   The lizard sets itself on fire
   Succulence passes from seashell to bedrock
   The monocle eye shuts in pain
   Habit-forming like the xylophone
   My little baby-celebs, how you all suffer
   But the nude works harder than you
   High-vaulted trees, our pricks stepping out
   Mussel-fossils
   Or velvet pipes alive & wet

At the Ramen Shop, A One-Act Play

Hungry, Thorn & Horn Satyr invites Red Bull Satyr for lunch. Various food trucks sit parked near the tomb.

THORN & HORN SATYR:

Let me buy you a bowl
Big stat in the Milky Way
The teapot stopped up
Milky broth
Stewed for days
A rose-by, a rosebud, a flower
noodle
Sliced pork Desiree
Hooked by noodles
Let me buy you a bowl
How hard how soft
I hope you like eating
Bowl to lap, lap to bowl

*(Steam rises from a fatty broth.
Murky deep and sweet, it holds
a tangle of scallion eyes.)*

RED BULL SATYR:

Down a tidy alley
To a faux-wood counter
Sauna-times chef's table
The entire egg
A mystery in spelling
A mystery in name
A tower of eggs
Yolks together, then apart
Shaken free of excess water
Under supple seaweed sheets
The squeal and sizzle
Of guzzling thorn & horn

Notes Toward a Fragmentary Theatre

At The Three Tombs, *a popular bar in Barcelona, Big Bear Satyr and Little Hunter Satyr unwind after a long day. They are not due at the playhouse until after first call, preferably soused, plunged entire in drink. Wineskins loose, flapping skin.*

BIG BEAR SATYR: Order me a drink
since the body invents
all kinds of new resistances.
Yes, order me a drink,
make it acidic, not too sweet.

LITTLE HUNTER SATYR: My dear one, hold on. *(dives deep into her pocket, clatter of winsome change)*
Think of an echo
as the original sound
since it leaves as first difference.

BIG BEAR SATYR: Instead of speaking in riddles,
let's watch the smoke rise
from these tombs,
and pray for our dear Antigone.
How will she ever escape?

LITTLE HUNTER SATYR: Tomb as ultimate archive.

BIG BEAR SATYR: All archives are gestures
of approximation. *(tips a flask, opens his purple-dark lips)*
Enough, order me a drink.

LITTLE HUNTER SATYR: Smoke as original voice.

BIG BEAR SATYR:	Did you know there's no entry for echo in the Princeton dictionary?
LITTLE HUNTER SATYR:	And sound has no beginning. It's useless to even look.

Big Bear Satyr Sends a Valentine, A One-Act Play

We see Big Bear Satyr,
drunk and happy,
turning and turning
in the yard, a dusty blow up.
His boot tips twisting
a bouquet of buttercups.

BIG BEAR SATYR: Terribly happy
In human taste
Let's meet same time-same place
In ill-fated human footage

A Silent Score

*We overhear Red Bull Satyr and Thorn & Horn Satyr
discussing origins. Perception a two-way
street in the amphitheater of loss—*

THORN & HORN SATYR: If I burn of fire,
                        imagine a theft, a crime,
                        a shortwave radio
                        en route to Rapallo.

RED BULL SATYR: If I burn of fire,
                        I'm the fire-breathing,
                        five-legged wolf slinking
                        into your unattended bed
                        after selling liters of premium
                        gasoline to your illiterate cousins.

                        *(Just then, the harbor beamed
                        a fresco of light. A steamy scene
                        depicted on the Cleveland vase
                        complete with two-headed snakes.)*

                        (Little Hunter Satyr walks onstage.)

                        (A volcano erupts.)

LITTLE HUNTER SATYR: Our bodies as sound chambers,
                        our skulls even. "The distinct
                        sensation of a voice coming
                        out from behind me."
                        Footfall on threshold.
                        The clunk and skunk.
                        The clatter of a common wall.

Scholia

The morning after a big party, the Satyrs find what looks like ancient papyri hidden inside a goat's costume. Before the 9th century, scholia *could refer to a choral society of imperial guards, warrior servants, or fire-breathing monks standing guard. Later, it came to mean commentary written alongside the margins of an ancient play.*

his bones
      buried
acres   black
salt
  outside
patio
monument
unearth

                            from the limestone shards
                               a satyr bas-relief

                            "Voices I am following
                           lead me to the margin."

a snowflake in Greece
or a lightning bolt, so to speak
both stirring awake the realm of the uncanny

cracks in the formula
a hanging foreskin

like the strange music under the earth
like the strange clarity of music
                               choral a living wall
an illustration of the action

Illumination, you mean   divine
protection

                        chorus like an echo
               perhaps nothing like Dionysus

?
Or just an   EMPTY HOLE

                   She does whatever she wants
as she should,
the twice-led life
often misunderstood

Adagia for a Sisterly Theatre

*The Satyrs receive the following instructions from an
anonymous source regarding their upcoming production,* The
Bakkhai. *They crowd around Big Bear Satyr and read over
his shoulder, the stench of wine on their breaths.*

Begin at the beginning,
also called *What Vanish*.

∞

The female body always half-way.

∞

The act of writing is the first
witness to the performance,
its author witness to the witness.

∞

The female body actual.
The female pure and raw and actually
livid in liveness—
a burning soundless flame.

∞

When staging *Hamlet*, Act V, Scene X,
make sure Laertes and Hamlet
miss the womb as tomb,
proving their sexual ownership of Ophelia
cannot be consummated.

∞

The female playwright reappearing—

∞

Writing as enactment.
Performance as re-enactment.
Actor as editor
or as re-discovered (hidden) (unannounced)
writer?

∞

For the echo,
Time is not theatrical,
it simply must exist.
If the echo touches Time,
it will destroy itself.

∞

The sister playwright must contend
with the mystery of her own
vanishing.

But If We Think of Origin

Onstage is a tomb, from which smoke rises.
Vine-shoots trailing off its limestone language.
The Satyrs reminisce of first beginnings.

[CHORAL ODE]

ALL: We gifted the drums to *The Bakkhai*
       The living vibration
       The livewire
       A pulsing constellation
       A living fire
       Kettledrums and tambourines
       Palace-miracles nourishing the young

       Milk – honey – wine

       Greekless Reader, find me in the Annex
       Writing notes on the wall
       Tinged in blue
       The world shakes topsy-turvy
       As if an earthquake
       Could settle matters

       Milk – honey – wine

       Instead of seeing first differences
       Train the eye to contour
       Open multiples of sameness
       Where we all agree
       That joy is the underside of sane
       And life, the here and now

A voice in the sky
Its celebration and song
The drunken caress

The Greek leaf
Teeming with
Headstrong longing
A green meadow
Coursing in joy

21c.

Little Hunter Satyr pens a love letter.

LITTLE HUNTER SATYR: A magic lantern
show set in the
wildflowers of west
Texas: reticence
itself. Stuck in
the Sublime,
the strum & thrum
of vocal cords.
Imaginary mount
-ains, or the felt
texture of talking,
a double con
-densation of
raw material,
your soft lips
the fluttering
shutter of
Morse codes,
the way the lace
veil hides
and reveals
just enough.

Little Hunter Satyr Throws Her Phone Into the Bristle-Grass (Epilogue)

The satyr play goes back to something
more primitive than a tragedy or comedy.
Phallic props, a zero lake, a hogged wineskin,

a flimflam snowjob. All lovers like heists.
A punch in slow motion is not a real punch.
In the grassland, near drums of beer,

we rake the bristle-grass to the tune
of the lost-ringing cell phone.
The highway, a dry cicada noise

messing with our heart-heads.
I roam the given landscape
in a Frenchman's peephole.

> *The nude one, the hairless*
> *one, dying in the grasses.*
> *New Romance, Vermont.*

Fate can't control all that's brought to ruin.

"BOLD SPEECH:" AN AFTERWORD

'Tis no disparagement to be a stranger, or so irksome to be an exile. The rain is a stranger to the earth, rivers to the Sea, Jupiter in Egypt, the Sun to us all. The Soul is an alien to the Body, a Nightingale to the air, a Swallow in an house, and Ganymede in Heaven, an Elephant at Rome, a Phoenix in India; and such things commonly please us best which are most strange, and come farthest off. – Robert Burton (*The Anatomy of Melancholy*)

Imagination creates reality, and as desire is a part of imagination, the world we desire is more real than the world we passively accept. – Northrop Frye (*Fearful Symmetry*)

Medea nunc sum: crevit ingenium malis.
[Now I am Medea: my genius has grown through evils.]
– Seneca

Poets and playwrights who have turned their art to the story of Medea have been among the most hallowed in world literature. Euripides, for example, in one of the earliest and certainly most famous treatments of Medea, dramatically portrayed a scorned woman whose belief in oaths turned to infanticide. Seneca, writing several centuries after Euripides and during the early years of the Roman Empire, shifted the focus of the play to Medea's anger, giving Medea a curse-inflamed opening soliloquy that set the tone for a monologic revenge tragedy. Ovid, whose dramatic version of the story unfortunately remains lost, eschewed the revenge plot in his verse-epic, *The Metamorphoses*, in favor of Medea's prodigious occult powers. While it's the shortest of the major classical adaptations of the Medea myth, Ovid's treatment has nevertheless significantly influenced post-classical poetry, specifically poetry of the English Renaissance, which in its Neo-Platonic variety frequently associated occult with poetic powers. As some critics have noted, Prospero's renunciation of his powers at the end of *The Tempest* (5.1.33-57) ironically echoes Medea's invocation of her dark powers in Book 7 of Ovid's poem.

The three versions of the Medea story mentioned above not only highlight its important literary genealogy, but also suggest that each version stands as a testament to the protean nature of myth. Although myth, according to Northrop Frye, employs conventional tropes, topoi, and storylines to create a "unified imaginative experience," the use of those poetic conventions by artists differ significantly.[1] Such room for aesthetic and thematic diversity allows the stories to be told afresh, which in turn allows myths to speak across generations.

Speaking to and engaging with Euripides, Ovid, and Seneca (among other sources) from the twenty-first century, Catherine Theis' *MEDEA* freely takes the story into new imaginative territory by embracing the myth's dark creative forces.[2] Just as Euripides chose to reimagine Greek tragedy through ordinary and lifelike rather than elevated tragic figures, Theis reconceptualizes the relationship between Medea and Jason (i.e., the "Husband") for the modern reader.[3] Not only does Theis change the primary setting from Corinth to Montana

---

[1] See *Northrop Frye on Milton and Blake* (University of Toronto Press, 2005).

[2] Two important adaptations of the Medea myth not mentioned above are Apollonius of Rhodes' *The Argonautika* and Ovid's epistle from Medea to Jason (XII) in *Heroides*.

[3] See "Murder in the Family – Medea and Others" by Jasper Griffin in *Looking at Medea* (Bloomsbury, 2015), edited by David Stuttard, p. 15.

and the ending from infanticide to mariticide, she also
provides the play with a different moral trajectory. Theis
doesn't seem as concerned with oaths, justice, or revenge,
but rather with the imagination. In this sense we
find a more Ovidian Medea in Theis' adaptation, one
that explores the relationship between language and
art. Medea's language rather than her occult powers
provides the play with its pyrotechnic dimension, setting
fire both to physical objects (e.g., the cabin) and the
imaginative life of its titular character. Like Clytemnestra
in Aeschylus' ruthless tragedy, *Agamemnon*, Theis'
Medea verbally and imaginatively dominates the play.
It seems that only the Milky Way, one of Theis' brilliant
additions to the play, can spar with Medea's preternatural
eloquence:

THE MILKY WAY

Heracles, of both heaven
and earth, sucks on Hera's breast
whose milk of kindness
sprays a starry chest.

And so we are thus born—
a spray of grace
across the nightly firmament.

MEDEA

Your glowing strands cast
filament after filament.
In the cataract of disaster,
a down-rushing of forms.
A curtain fall of blue flowers.

The lyrical intensity of this verse, like the "glowing

strands" of the Milky Way viewed in the American West, glitters and glimmers, suggesting Medea's linguistic connection to higher powers. "In a down-rushing of forms," Medea speaks a language that binds imagination to its celestial origin, the heavens. (Such an affinity between infinity and imagination illustrates what Edmund Burke would identify in its obscurity as the sublime.) As the play's language emphatically suggests, Medea has more in common with the Chorus of Flames and the Milky Way than with her Husband.

Equating Medea's language with imagination and the sublime highlights fundamental issues that separate her from her Husband. Theis' Medea is wickedly intelligent, abundantly imaginative, and highly attuned to the natural world. Her Husband, however, lacks all the aforementioned qualities. The scene that perhaps best captures their difference occurs post-conflagration, when Medea, soliloquizing, walks by her Husband on the payphone and repeats where he leaves off:

> Time works us against us
> …
> I can't fall back asleep. I wait for water.
> But there's pressure inside the mountain.
> I'm afraid it's transforming into a volcano.
> All the birds have flown. Even the birds know
> it's time to head out on sulfur fume.
> Where do you put bold voices?
> The wish for bold speech never escapes me.

While the cabin fire in the previous scene suggests a proto-shift or what Aristotle would call a reversal (*peripeteia*) in the play ("This is your midnight pilgrimage, isn't it? / You did this."), the soliloquy fundamentally illustrates not only Medea's moral and aesthetic superiority to her Husband, but also her courage not to "fall back asleep"; that is, return to an imaginative and erotic *ennui*. Instead, as the "pressure inside the mountain" builds, she allows her Husband's "unbloodied instruction" to assist her moral language (*lexis*), which speaks for all those who have been wronged, misunderstood, and, most sadly, neglected.

The Greeks have a provocative term for "bold speech": *parrhêsia* (*par* = "all" and *r[h]esia* = "speech"). The term generally means "to speak everything" or "to speak freely" and suggests taking a risk by not hiding the truth. As Foucault argues in one of the most influential readings of the concept: "For there to be *parrhêsia* [. . .] the subject must be taking some kind of risk [. . .] *Parrhêsia* consists in telling the truth without concealment, reserve, empty manner of speech, or rhetorical ornament which might encode or hide it. 'Telling all' is then: telling the truth without hiding any part of it, without hiding it behind anything."[4] In Euripides' late play *Ion* (ca. 414 BCE), *parrhêsia* plays an important role in establishing whether a God or a human possesses the right to speak the truth. Many additional plays by Euripides engage the concept of *parrhêsia*, but few scholars seem to discuss the concept in relation to *Medea*. Theis, however, emphatically shifts the action of the play to focus on Medea's parrhesiastic language of courage, truth, and beauty, perhaps the trifecta of her moral world. "Bold speech" thus becomes Medea's means of being in and resisting a world that has extinguished (or rendered meaningless) these concepts through acts of betrayal and infidelity.

---

[4] See *The Courage of Truth (The Governance of Self and Others II): Lectures at the Collège de France 1983-1984* (Palgrave, 2011).

As with all great tragic figures, Medea grows, changes, and becomes more fully herself in the course of Theis' play. With the help of a voicemail "recognition" (*anagnorisis*) scene, a scene which importantly provides the necessary psychological realism to warrant the "use [of] love / to further love," Medea embraces her role as "creative force," breaking through the "metal gate" and dislodging the "shackle[s]" of her Husband's cruelty. The play's dénouement highlights just how significant an education Medea undergoes in the action of the play, depicting a woman's ecstatic speech "unprotected by the gods / but swarmed in butterflies":

> Nothing is ever an accident,
> the bad fit of creative force,
> the metal gate, the sliding shackle.
> I killed, I may kill again.
> But for now, choreograph me
> into the trees' canopy—
> pine needle feet in loam-top brush
> Liar, wormweed—I drink what I please,
> my new life unprotected by the gods
> but swarmed in butterflies.

Perhaps due to Medea's association with infanticide, most classical and modern adaptations of the Medea myth seem to privilege the sensational over the moral, giving Medea's murderous plot center stage. This trend tends to avoid both Medea's proto-feminism and her genuinely creative powers. Theis' Medea, however, explores this neglected dimension of the myth by foregrounding Medea's "good" powers of art and song. Consequently, Theis recuperates a figure whose occult/witch stigma has often placed her with Circe and Sycorax (from Shakespeare's *The Tempest*) as a marginalized female threat. Theis' Medea takes issue with the very notion of female silence and replaces it with a roaring sound, which, as Medea says in her final lines, is an "immortal ecstatic fire."

Steven Aaron Minas
Santa Monica, California

STEVEN AARON MINAS was born in Texas and grew up in Arizona. After attending the University of Arizona where he studied English and Classics, Steven received a Master's in English Literature from Georgetown University. Steven is currently pursuing a Ph.D. in English Literature at the University of Southern California. While his scholarly interests primarily lie at the intersection of Renaissance poetry and moral philosophy, he nevertheless spends much of his time reading widely in modern experimental poetry and poetics.

ACKNOWLEDGMENTS

Grateful acknowledgment is made to the following publications in which the poems of this book first appeared: *1913 a journal of forms*, *POOL*, and Kelsey Street Press' "Featured Work by Emerging Writers" series.

Grateful acknowledgment is also made to Robert Eric Shoemaker and the *Poetry Is Theatre Festival*, where a production of *MEDEA* ran in June 2016 at the Comfort Station in Chicago, Illinois.

Many thanks to the Del Amo Foundation for the generous support.

Many thanks to Megan J. Pryce for her exacting vision on the design of this vibrant book.

Many thanks and admiration to Tyler Crumrine for his editorial prescience and innovation. Your commitment to the arts is breathtaking—you are a marvel. Thank you.

Many thanks to my family, teachers, and friends who push me into dangerous fields of extravagant possibility: Sandra Alcosser, Emily Anderson, John Beer, Janalynn Bliss, Joseph Dane, Lesley Guthrie, Elissa Hobfoll, Mark Irwin, Mark Levine, John Kaufman, Joanna Klink, Susan McCabe, Radka Opalka, Shelley Roth, Diane Rayor, Robert Eric Shoemaker, Jessica Savitz, Bruce Smith, Jared Stanley, David St. John, Cole Swensen, and Elizabeth Theis. Special thanks to my parents, William and Maria Luisa Theis, who make everything possible with their cloud of warm, harmonious, and literate love.

I am eternally grateful to Aaron Minas. Without you, there is no story.

CATHERINE THEIS is a poet who writes plays. Her first book of poems is *The Fraud of Good Sleep* (Salt Modern Poets, 2011), followed by her chapbook, *The June Cuckold, a tragedy in verse* (Convulsive, 2012). She has received various fellowships and awards, most notably from the Illinois Arts Council and the Del Amo Foundation. Theis' scholarly work explores the relationship between H.D.'s classical translations and her poetics.

Oh. this is what it feels like to not have a secret.